UoLearn™
Easy 4 me 2 learn

Also by Angela Hepworth: Studying for your future
ISBN 978-1-84937-047-9

Order books from your favorite bookseller or direct from www.uolearn.com

Preparing for your Future: Study skills to get ready for university, college and work. Choose your course, study skills, action planning, time management, write a CV, employability and career advice.

Published by: Universe of Learning Ltd, reg number 6485477, Lancashire, UK
www.uolearn.com, support@uolearn.com

ISBN 978-1-84937-085-1

Other editions: ebook pdf format 978-1-84937-090-5

ebook epub format 978-1-84937-091-2

Thanks and Dedication

Thanks:

I would like to thank all my fellow students as the opportunity to teach you has given me the knowledge and expertise to write this book.

I would also like to thank all my friends and colleagues who continually help me to stay focused when working towards the goals that I set for myself. My heartfelt thanks goes to Margaret Greenhall, my editor, as without the constant support my books would still be in the draft stages. Thank you so much for all your dedicated time in making the books real.

Dedication:

I dedicate this book to all my close friends and family who continually support me through life's challenges and who encourage me to have a positive outlook in everything that I do.

I also dedicate this book to my dad who has left behind his strength and wisdom that has made me such a determined individual with the philosophy:

>*'You only get out of life what you put in.'*

>*'You reap what you sew.'*

Thank you Dad for this gift.

Angela Hepworth

Angela has over twenty five years' experience teaching in Further and Higher Education and also teaching 14-19 year olds in schools and colleges.

At present she is a Senior Lecturer in the department of Sport and Physical Activity at Edge Hill University in Ormskirk, Lancashire specializing in study skills, personal development and research methods. She also specializes in life coaching and getting people to where they aspire to be in their lives.

Angela has worked extensively with students to support them in developing their academic skills, which has helped them to be successful. She encourages the students to work towards their goals which will allow them to develop themselves personally and professionally.

It is hoped this book will help students to prepare themselves to go to university and also equip them with the skills required to start out on their degree programmes.

Many of the exercises have printable versions which can be downloaded from www.uolearn.com.

Contents

List of Exercises

Chapter 1:
Choosing which university or college is best for you

"The secret of getting ahead is getting started.
The secret of getting started is breaking your complex
overwhelming tasks into small manageable tasks,
and then starting on the first one." Mark Twain

Chapter 1:
Choosing which university or college is best for you

As you will be spending the next three or four years studying at the University of your choice, it is very important that you will be happy with the environment, the facilities, the resources, the teaching staff and the other students on your course.

In order for you to make the right decision it is always a good idea to make contact with each of the universities you would like to study at. Thoroughly investigate their websites and prospectuses. Ask their admissions team when their open days or visit days are and if you can't make an open day ask if you can come on an individual visit. Often open days are planned at the weekend so it won't affect your attendance at school or college.

To help you to decide on which courses to study you need to discuss your options with your tutors at school or college and they will tell you whether they think you have enough subject knowledge or specific skills to go onto a degree programme.

If you are a mature or international student you will have to ask some very different questions as to whether the qualifications you've got will count towards getting a place on the degree programme, or if the qualifications you have gained from abroad have the same equivalence in your chosen country. You may have to do an access course to that particular programme, an entrance exam, a reflective piece of writing or write an assignment on a chosen topic. You also need to investigate any visa restrictions.

If you don't feel you will achieve the grades to get into university, then speak with your tutors at school or college. They may advise you to do a Foundation degree or to reapply to do your school exams so you can achieve higher grades.

If you have your sights set on attending university to gain a degree, it may not always be straight forward. It is usually achievable, it just takes some people longer or some people may have to go down a different route. Have a look at distance study providers like the Open University.

What's important is that when you get there you have chosen the right course.

Course choices

During your school years you will have completed a list of options of subjects to study. As you progress through these subjects you should have started to get a flavour for the types of subjects you are interested in and that you are good at.

Once you have established the kinds of subjects you are interested in you can look at the possible choices for continuing on in higher education. It's a good idea to have a look at the prospectuses for quite a few universities as they offer many subjects that are not available at school. Think carefully about what careers a course will lead you to. If you have a careers advice center at school make good use of it.

> **Case study: Mature entry to university**
>
> Jo had family problems and had to leave home and school at 16. Later on she decided to return to study and started an Open University degree. Her dream was to be a dentist. She completed the equivalent for the first two years of a science degree and then applied to a local university for entry to the dental school. Her qualifications were now good enough but she was initially refused a place because she'd just passed her thirtieth birthday. She appealed and after a lot of hard work persuaded the admissions team to offer her a place. She now owns and runs a very successful group of three dental practices.

The key questions you have to consider when planning your future are:

✓ Do I want to work with adults or children?

✓ Do I want to work indoors or outdoors?

✓ Do I want to work days, evenings, weekends or shift work?

✓ What potential earnings would I like?

✓ What are my long term career ambitions?

By answering these questions you may gain a better idea of the type of career you want to pursue (see exercise 28 for a longer set of questions). This should then lead you to asking what subjects do I need to study to be able to gain employment in that area. Have a look at specialist magazines in your field of study like New Scientist, Nursing Times, Archeology Magazine etc. Just search for your main topic and magazine and you'll find several to look at.

Make sure you look at the universities website in detail. It should have staff profiles for the course you wish to study and what levels of expertise they have. You may also want to check whether the university has a research center. This will also inform you about the kinds of research the university and department are involved with. The university may be involved in research with partner institutions all over the world. All this will help you to develop your research knowledge and create further opportunities for you in the field of employability. By doing your own research into the different universities you will be able to identify what other opportunities the university can provide eg. work placements or international exchanges.

Your own careers department and specialist tutors at your school can help you with all this. Try and have a basic idea of what occupation or career you would like to work in. Chapter 4 will help you to do this.

*** Exercise 1: Where and what do I want to study? ***

Course choice:

If you want to think about your career choice then have a look at exercise 28. Remember that people often have a series of different careers now rather than one career for life so you are only thinking about your first career.

Universities offer far more courses than you've been able to study at school so firstly get a range of prospectuses and look through to see if there is anything you haven't already considered.

- ✓ Am I interested in the topic?
- ✓ What is the structure of the degree?
- ✓ Can I do it part time?
- ✓ What opportunities would there be for a Masters course or postgraduate research in this area?
- ✓ What types of jobs do people get after the course?
- ✓ What is the employment rate at the end of the course?
- ✓ What is the completion rate for the course?
- ✓ How many hours a week will I be in classes?
- ✓ How will the course be assessed?
- ✓ How many years will the course take?
- ✓ Are there opportunities for work placements on the course?
- ✓ Will there be opportunities to work with international students?
- ✓ How long is the turnaround of marking assignments so I can receive feedback?
- ✓ How accessible are the staff to help me with my studies?
- ✓ How well equipped is the department?
- ✓ What is the national and international reputation of the department?

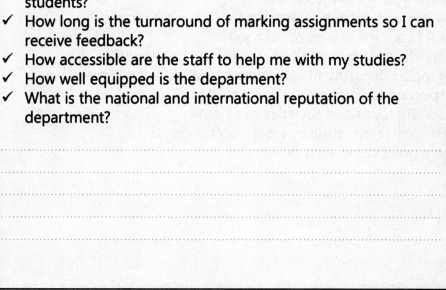

University choice:

- ✓ Will I live away from home?
- ✓ Can I afford to live away from home?
- ✓ Can I commute to university easily?
- ✓ Can I keep my part-time job whilst still studying?
- ✓ What size of town do I want to live in?
- ✓ How many students are on the course and how many in the whole university?
- ✓ What is the national and international reputation of the university?
- ✓ Will I have to support myself with a part-time job?
- ✓ What opportunities are there for part time work near the university? (Look for places that have other major industries, particularly tourism.)
- ✓ If I am going to travel to the university, how much will it cost?
- ✓ How much will it cost to park my car?
- ✓ Will public transport get me there on time?
- ✓ Will I have to walk from the train station or bus station?
- ✓ Will my accommodation be far away from where I am studying?
- ✓ What's the crime rate like near the university and its accommodation?
- ✓ What will the living accommodation be like?
- ✓ What days will I need to attend?
- ✓ How much will the fees be?
- ✓ Will I have to pay out for field trips as part of my course?
- ✓ Will I have any more additional costs on top of my tuition fees? e.g. sports kit, books, materials, protective clothing, outdoor wear.
- ✓ Will I have a personal tutor?
- ✓ Will my personal tutor be the same for the whole course?
- ✓ Who will I ask for a reference for a job?
- ✓ What are the employability statistics for the university?
- ✓ What support departments are there e.g. study skills, careers, library?
- ✓ What sporting facilities are there for students?
- ✓ What social groups and societies can I join?
- ✓ Are there any recent student satisfaction surveys?
- ✓ Are there good computing facilities?

....

....

....

....

Scholarships

The university of your choice may have scholarships available for you to apply for before you start at the university after being offered a definite place. The scholarship scheme awards offer a student a sum of money. This can be in the form of a one off payment or payment at the beginning of each academic year. Scholarships may be rewards for excellence, financial background, sporting skills etc.. Make sure you understand exactly what the criteria are so that you can make your application more likely to succeed. Some of the scholarships may be in the form of a book token or a substantial amount that will contribute towards your studies. Find out about them as soon as you have decided on your university as they may have very tight deadlines for applications.

Once you are on course ask your tutors about scholarship schemes that are run by that particular university and again tell the staff that you are interested in being put forward for an award.

The university may also offer bursaries and other hardship fund facilities in which students can ask for help towards housing costs and living accommodation. Short term loans may be available and grants to help students who are going through hardship because of personal circumstances.

It is well worth discussing your options available with your student representative on your course, the student union, student information center staff or your personal tutor who can recommend the best person to help you. Always ask - they can always say no. It will also give you a feeling for how friendly and supportive the staff are.

Applying to go to University

Lots of people have very similar qualifications and therefore your personal statement is the one thing that distinguishes your application from the rest. This is why your personal statement for your application to university is a very important part of the application process and you should take time and care when writing it.

If you choose a particular place to study and it meets all your criteria then it's important to write an outstanding personal statement which will help you get the offer of a place. You need to use it as a sales letter to tell the admissions tutor why you deserve the place above all the rest of the applicants.

This exercise will give some options as to what to include in your final application. The more you write, the easier it becomes when you allow your mind to become creative.

*** Exercise 2: Writing your personal statement ***

Write a paragraph on each of the following, this will help you to write a personal statement.

What are your career aspirations?

What do you want to achieve once you finish your degree?

Why have you chosen to study this course at this university?

Why are you suitable for the course?

How do your current studies relate to the degree that you have chosen?

Tell me about yourself.

Have you participated in any work experience?

What do you regard as your key strengths?

Write about your skills and achievements and any awards that you are working towards or have gained already.

Do you participate in a sporting activity?

Are you a member of a team?

Think about how your hobbies, interests and social activities demonstrate your skills and abilities. If there's anything that relates to your course or to the skills needed to complete a higher education course then include it. The more evidence you give the better. Remember to mention any attributes that make you stand out from all the rest.

Write about any work experience you have had and the skills you gained whilst working. This can be paid or unpaid work or again any voluntary experience you have done.

If you are a mature student you may want to write about your life experiences and the challenges you have faced.

International students may wish to comment on why you want to study in their chosen country. How can you demonstrate that you can complete a degree course that will be mainly taught and examined in a different language? You may want to mention if you have travelled outside your country and used other languages.

If you feel you will need specialist support at university it may be a good idea to discuss this on your personal statement. Most universities have specialist centers to help and provide a wide range of services to help you with all aspects of your university life. Some of the things that might be available are: specialist equipment and resources, trained staff who will help to learn how to cope with your assignments, support groups, free or cheap accessibility software etc.. There may even be grants available for computer equipment. You can contact them directly before you've applied to see how they might be able to help you.

Getting organized for your study

Before you start at University it's important that you familiarize yourself with what resources you are going to need. This may include a lap top, mobile phone, separate hard drive for storing large amounts of data, pen drive, camera, box files to store journal articles, text books, pens, paper, mathematical instruments, outdoor clothing for field trips, sportswear for sports courses, saucepans, plates, cups (remember to get enough for your friends who'll visit) etc.. These can be very costly items and should be considered in your planning.

Write a list of everything you might need for study and living and then add as many as you can to your birthday and Christmas lists. Also let friends and family know what you're looking for - you'll be surprised a how many will give you spare things they have.

Make sure you get your own insurance - usually student accommodation does not cover your property. You might be able be covered by your parent's policy - it's always worth asking.

Some ideas for the basics:

Check what facilities are available where you're going to be living first.

Saucepans, frying pan, wooden spoons, spatula, sharp small knife, knives, forks, spoons, teaspoons, mugs, glasses, plates, bowls, chopping board, mixing bowl, colander, kettle, toaster

Duvet, 2 duvet covers, pillows, pillow cases

Pens, paper, ruler, eraser, pencils, desktidy, lined paper, plain paper, folders, calculator, box files, in/out tray, stapler, sellotape, post-its, computer, printer, 4 way power socket, phone, chargers

Washing powder, washing up liquid, cloths for cleaning, toilet paper, kitchen towel

Toothpaste, toothbrush, soap, shampoo, any medication, nail clippers, razor, flannel, hand towel, 2 large towels

Tea, coffee, sugar, biscuits

Accommodation and travel

Living in halls at the university isn't always the easiest or cheapest option and many universities have limited availability. Most university towns or cities start to advertise student lets or accommodation as early as January for the following September intake. It may be worth a visit into the town center or have a look at estate agents and local paper websites to see if there is accommodation available. There will be an accommodation team at the university. They offer advice on accommodation within the university and they will be able to give you advice on renting in the area of the university. This may mean sharing a house with other students or using a room in a family house. Always check to see if the utility bills (gas, electricity etc.) are included as part of your rent as this will be another factor when working out your finances. This needs to be taken into consideration when planning for university. Don't rent without visiting the property and walking around at night to check that you feel safe.

Some students who travel into the university forget to take into account how much travel arrangements cost if you live away from the university. For the first few weeks it can be expensive until you can find someone to car share with.

If you are likely to have very early or late classes then you need to check the timetables for public transport to make sure you can get there on time. It becomes unpleasant when travelling home in the dark if you have to stand around at train and bus stations. It's a good idea to live within walking or cycling distance of the university and benefit from everything that happens around the community of the campus.

More often students share accommodation. It is important that you meet the people you are going to be sharing a house with. Sometimes these arrangements don't always work out and you could have already signed a contract until the end of the academic year. If this is the case you will still be liable to pay the rent until the end of your contract.

Handling your finances

Most students struggle with their finances when they first attend university as it is probably the first time they have managed their money on their own. For many students it's likely that you will have bigger bills than income. Depending on which country you live in there will be different fee structures and loans available but always visit the student finance office as soon as you can to get any available help.

Even if you know there is no way you can get through without a big loan it is best to know exactly what is coming in and going out every month.

You need to have a spread sheet with incomings and outgoings on it and it needs to be honest and list everything. Yes you may be getting into debt but you need to contain it to the minimum it has to be.

Remember, if you work, to find out what tax has been taken off. You may even be due a tax refund at the end of the year, especially if you didn't work a full year in a job. Read up on the tax liabilities for your country you'll be surprised as to what you might be allowed to offset against the tax and you'll need to keep receipts to be able to do it.

You can download an example excel speadsheet from www. uolearn.com

Headings for your spread sheet:

Incomings:

Loan, Grant, Parents, Work, Savings, Other

Outgoings

Fees, Rent, Tax, Food, Electricity, Gas, Water, Internet access, Telephone, Building rates, Insurance, Toiletries, Daily travel, Travel home, Books, Supplies for course, Stationary, Clothes, Shoes, Household items, Entertainment, Other

How University differs from school

Once you start at university you will notice the lecturers have a completely different attitude compared to your school teachers. The responsibility shifts from the teachers telling you what to do to you taking control of your study. You have to learn to be proactive and ask for help as the tutors have so many students they might not know you need help.

As there are so many students with so many specific individual needs the university provides support mechanisms in order to help students with issues they may be facing. You should be allocated a personal tutor on your course who will have the responsibility of making sure you settle in to the university and also that you are on track with all your work. There will often be a central student support department that can help you with a range of issues. Visit them early in your first year so you know exactly what they can help you with.

The university or your course may have an attendance policy and it will be up to your personal tutor or module leader to ensure that you adhere to the attendance policy. Some universities don't have attendance policies. However, a register may still be taken at every lecture and every seminar. It is up to you to take responsibility for your own learning. This is where university is different from school. At school it is the teacher's responsibility, at university it is your own.

It's really important to let the university or your module tutor know about your absences. If your absences are for a genuine reason then if you miss a deadline for an assignment or an exam you can claim mitigating circumstance and you may be granted extra time or allowed to have your work considered.

Notices will be put up on noticeboards, websites, V.L.E's (virtual learning environments - the university online teaching software) for you to follow. It's your responsibility to find the information. If you are unsure you should ask your personal tutor. Don't rely on what other students tell you as they might have got it wrong. Universities are very strict on deadlines for work, so if your work is late you will get a zero grade and this will have an impact on your overall mark for that module.

Most universities won't accept you back onto the course for the following year if you have 2 failed modules, you may have to come back as a part time student. It is better if you try hard all year and ask for guidance if you are unsure of anything. Don't leave issues until the last minute. It is important that you achieve high grades from the outset.

Many students get their biggest wake up call after Christmas in the second year of their studies. That's when they suddenly realize they have to improve otherwise they risk getting a low degree classification.

It would be better to start in the right way from the beginning with good habits and that's what the next chapter of the book covers.

Notes:

Chapter 2:
Skills needed for success
in higher education

"Planning is bringing the future into the present so that you can do something about it now." Alan Lakein

Chapter 2:
Skills needed for success in higher education

The learning cycle:

EXPERIENCING
Taking part in the
learning activity

REFLECTING
Reviewing and analyzing the
experience and the results

THEORIZING
Integrating the experience with
both your own and
other people's views of the world

PLANNING
Planning any changes
and new strategy

The above cycle is known as the Kolb or learning cycle. For effective learning people need to undertake all four parts. You need to take part in learning experiences, reflect on the experience and connect the experience to everything else you've learned then plan your next learning experience. Traditionally degrees concentrated on helping people to learn the knowledge and skills needed for a particular career. Most courses had very little about the learning process itself and reflecting on how you learn and becoming a better learner. However, in the modern world, most people change careers several times. So you have to develop systems for coordinating your own personal development. Being able to reflect on your experience helps this process. If you can engage with all four parts of the learning cycle it will enhance your learning.

Planning

To keep your life in some kind of order it is important to have achievable goals and also to create action plans. Planning and goal setting will help you to become more successful in your study and career.

It is important when you are planning to go to university that you devise an action plan and state what dates and deadlines you have for your application form to be in to the relevant organizations.

This can sometimes be the most time consuming part of your preparation but once it is completed you can then see exactly what else you have left to do.

Writing action plans for all major assignments will help you to be success at university.

It is a good way to practice your time management skills to reach the deadlines and targets you set for yourself but to also work to a timescale in readiness for the next three years at university whereby you may have three or four projects in at the same time and exam stress on top.

Following are some examples of action plans.

Action plan to apply for University.

Name of university:

Date to be completed: Friday 4th October

Time scale	Action	Key points	Date completed	Notes
Mon 19th August	Download application form			
Mon 2nd September.	Rewrite CV			
Tues 10th September	Check that my references are up to date, send emails or tel to ask permission to use referees names	Need to get 1 new referee as Mrs White left the school		
Mon 16th September	Write personal statement	Rem to include examples of team work, time management and leadership		
Sat 21st September	Fill in application form			
Mon 30th September	Proofread all materials	Read slowly and several times		
Weds 2nd October	Get mum and Mr Smith to check forms			
Friday 4th October	Get form in	Celebrate		

Action plan to complete a 2,000 word assignment.

Title of assignment:

Date to be completed: Thurs 24th March

Time scale	Action	Key points	Date completed	Notes
Week 1 Start date: Mon 28th Feb	Go to library for key reading take out relevant books. Print off the journal articles. Write plan for assignment.	Some books are only on 1 week loan. Read first and return. Show plan to tutor in next seminar.		
Week 2 Date: Mon 7th March Weds/Fri and Sunday afternoon.	Write introduction. Start reading books and articles for key literature and quotes to back up arguments. Aim to write 500 words.	Ask Ben if we can go out on Tues not Weds so I can work through into the evening.		
Week 3 Date: Mon 14th March Mon/Thurs and Sat	Write main body of the assignment. Aim to write 1000 words.	Working Tues, Weds, Fri so will only have Mon and Thurs evenings free. Go to bed straight after shifts at 10.		
Week 4: Date: Mon 21st March	Write summary. Read through and check it answers the question. Check for errors and make corrections. Hand in on 24th.			

*** Exercise 3: Action planning

Complete an action plan for an aspect of your course, this could be getting application forms in, an assignment, revision, team activity, job application, a project etc.

You can download blank versions of this grid from www.uolearn.com.

Action plan for:

Date to start:

Date to be completed:

Time scale	Action	Key points	Date complete	Notes

Reflection

Throughout your life and through school or college you will have gone through different experiences. By having a system to reflect on what has happened you'll learn more from each activity.

You may be asked as part of your course at school or college to keep a reflective log, a reflective journal or write a reflective report. You may have been asked to write down the thoughts you went through during an experience.

When you write reflectively you have to look back on the process that you went through and then decide what you would do differently if you were to do something similar in the future.

Reflection Questions

➢ What activity/event experience did you go through?
➢ Would you go through the process in exactly the same way if you did something similar in the future?
➢ What did you learn from carrying out the process in the way that you did?
➢ What advice would you give to yourself if you had to go through the process again?

Reflective practice, reflective practitioner, reflective log, reflective action plan, reflective diary and reflective journal; these are all key words that allow the writer to write in the first person. "I did this." 'I felt this." You need to describe both what happened and describe how it made you feel and how you would approach the same issue again.

This kind of writing is different from academic writing which doesn't allow you to write in the first person, you may only write in the third person (phrases such as: the researcher, according to Brown, Brown states that etc.).

You may be asked as part of your course to keep a reflective log or journal which you may write in everyday or every week for a short or long period of time. This can have a formal title at many universities such as PDP (personal development planning) and may even be credited towards your course.

You may also be asked to contribute to an online blog or discussion page which a select group have been invited to join. This is a good way to share experiences and challenges that you may be having. You can support each other and help to alleviate tension or problems when reading other people's reflective journals.

*** Exercise 4: Choose a recent experience you had, maybe learning to drive or taking your exams. ***

What did you do?

....
....
....

Would you go through the process in exactly the same way if you did something similar in the future?

....
....
....

What did you learn from carrying out the process in the way that you did?

....
....
....

What advice would you give yourself if you had to go through the process again?

....
....
....

Time Management

When we think about how much time can be wasted being non-productive, it is important that we plan our time effectively. Particularly, when you are doing a degree programme and you have deadlines to meet as well as juggling busy social lives and part time jobs and family.

One thing that is important to realize is that when there are too many things on the to-do list it is virtually impossible to stay focused.

Here are ten time saving suggestions:

1. Adopt mindmapping or concept maps (see later) for all your notes taken in lectures

2. Save time by reading weeks in advance the materials you need for your assignments

3. Keep your notes in one particular place to avoid having to look through pages and pages of subject material

4. Use a word limit to focus your energies

5. Avoid duplicating effort

6. Action plan each assignment

7. Action plan your exam revision timetable

8. Action plan your week

9. Set yourself a daily goal

10. Everyday say to yourself, "The purpose of the day is......."

Managing your Time

➢ Be aware of your own time management
➢ Make a note of how much time it takes you to complete each type of study task
➢ Take into account that many aspects of study take longer than expected
➢ Schedule time for unforeseen events
➢ Schedule time for relaxation and leisure

*** Exercise 5: Workflow diary ***

Many people just do not know how long it takes them to complete simple repetitive tasks.

Either:

Keep a diary for 3 days noting how long you take to do everything.
or
Add any more tasks you can think of then time the following list, you'll be amazed how long things take.

Task	Time (mins)
Make a hot drink	
Read 10 pages of a typical text book	
Type 200 words	
Find a useful website about one of your recent lectures	
Travel to a class	
Do your grocery shopping	

*** Exercise 6: How well do you manage your time? ***

Rate yourself on a scale of 1:awful to 5:excellent for the following:

	1	2	3	4	5
Do you usually turn up on time?	☹	○	😐	○	☺
Do you keep most appointments?	☹	○	😐	○	☺
Do you manage to fit in most of the things that you need to do?	☹	○	😐	○	☺
Do you get most things done without a last minute panic?	☹	○	😐	○	☺
Do you meet dead lines?	☹	○	😐	○	☺
Do you set time aside to relax?	☹	○	😐	○	☺
Do you use your time efficiently?	☹	○	😐	○	☺
Do you get on with tasks as soon as you get them?	☹	○	😐	○	☺
Can you find things quickly on your desk?	☹	○	😐	○	☺
Did you get everything done you needed to last week?	☹	○	😐	○	☺
Do you keep your diary up to date?	☹	○	😐	○	☺
Total					

Add up your total score:

10-25, you need to seriously look at your time management - you're working very inefficiently. You need to reappraise how you work and write an action plan for change. Each week pick one area of time management to work on, maybe decluttering your work environment or making a system for meeting your deadlines.

26-45, You're not working very efficiently and there is room for improvement. Pick 2 things from the list and work on them over the next week.

46-55, You've got great time management skills.

*** Exercise 7: Time planning - prioritizing ***

Draw up a priority setting checklist:

1. Write a list of everything you have to do.

2. Underline essential tasks in one color and items that can wait in another color.

3. Identify the most urgent item on the list.

4. Work out the best way this task can be approached.

5. Only focus on that one essential item, the rest can wait, otherwise you will bombard your brain and not achieve anything.

6. Work out how long you can spend on the urgent item to get the task completed before you can move onto the next task on your list.

7. Enter each essential task into your timetable or diary.

8. Avoid the things that take away your concentration levels, such as internet, television, mobile phone or other people. Music can help concentration but not if you're shouting out the words to the song!

Task	Priority

*** Exercise 8: Time planning - weekly planner ***

Another good way to plan out your time is to draw up a timetable of the week with 7 rows 3 columns. You can also buy diaries that have a week to view on a two page spread.

Fill the timetable in with everything that you do in your life for one week and see where you can free up some time to fit in study and revision time.

Obviously if you have to work part time as well you can't change the time that you go to work. You will then be able to see a pattern emerging that you tend to get some free time maybe on a Saturday or a Sunday afternoon.

	Morning	Afternoon	Evening
Monday			
Tuesday			
Wednesday			
Thursday			
Friday			
Saturday			
Sunday			

Your Work Environment

Once you get started on your course it is really important to choose your work environment very carefully as you may work better in one place rather than another. It may be that you can only work well in a library atmosphere or perhaps in your own room. Make sure you choose a place where you can avoid distraction. You must have comfort for your back, legs and shoulders, somewhere warm and somewhere you have access to drinking and toilet facilities.

A very important aspect of time management is to make sure your work environment is organized. If your desk is cluttered and disorganized not only will you waste time but also you'll get into a bad mood hunting for your stapler for the twentieth time this week. Some people like to have everything neat and filed away all the time, others need to see all of what they are working on at once. If you are one of the latter then make sure you have a large pen pot or set of in-trays for all your equipment like stapler, blue tack etc. and get into the habit of using them and returning them. Once a week or at the end of each major assignment clear your desk and tidy everything up, ready to start the next piece of work that is due.

One of the ways you can keep all your work organized is to invest in some box files. For each of your modules you can start by putting your module handbooks into the box file. Every time you download a journal or chapter of a book which is relevant to your study, add it to the box along with all of your lecture notes, You can keep all the materials together and this way you will know where everything is. This will also help you for the future as all your module boxes can be stored in order and each one will contain all your work for a particular course. When it comes to the final year of study and you have to submit your final piece of work or dissertation you already have great habits.

Goal Setting

If you don't know where you are going, how do you ever expect to get there!

In everything that we do in life we must set clear achievable goals for ourselves.

These may be short term, medium term or long term.

A short term goal may be achievable in one day, one week or one month.

A medium term goal may be achieved over a period of two to six months and long term goals are usually over a period of six months to ten years.

Inspirational speakers and writers worldwide talk about goal setting and focusing in on the energy to achieve that goal. My life coach once said to me that if you want to achieve a goal you have to do something about it every day. Chip, chip, chip away and you will get there I promise you.

Examples to inspire you may be:

- Starting your own business
- Get the best grade possible in your course
- Improving your writing skills
- Becoming a professional footballer
- Becoming a better coach
- Becoming a newsreader
- Travelling the world
- Finishing your degree
- Undertake some management training
- Learn to organize time more efficiently
- Finish masters' degree
- Learn yoga
- Go to the gym three times a week
- Eat more healthily

Case study: Life time achievements

When he was 15, John Goddard wrote a list of 127 dreams to achieve in his life. It wasn't just ordinary things there were some things that seemed impossible at the time (it was written in 1940) and included a visit to the moon. He has accomplished 109 out of that list. Including:

Explore: the Nile, the Amazon and the Congo rivers.

Climb: Mt Kenya, Mt Rainer, Mt Fuji

Photograph: Victoria falls, Yosemite falls,

Retrace the steps of Marco Polo and Alexander the Great

Visit: The Great Wall of China, Easter Island, The Taj Mahal

Swim in: Lake Superior, Lake Victoria, Lake Nicaragua

Accomplish: Write a book, Publish in National Geographic, Run a mile in 5 mins, Learn French, Spanish and Arabic, Make a telescope, Watch a cremation ceremony in Bali, Marry and have children, Land off and take off from an aircraft carrier, Circumnavigate the globe.

To see the full list visit: http://www.johngoddard.info/life_list.htm

Goals differ from dreams in that they are based on your knowledge of where you are and the journey you can definitely travel. Dreams are what you hope to achieve in your lifetime but you may not currently have the resources to start the journey.

Examples:

Goals: Complete my essay by next Monday.
To get a first class honors degree.

Dreams: To walk on Mars.
To fly across the country in a hot air balloon.

*** Exercise 9: What are your dreams? ***

What if you had completely unlimited money?
What will you really love to have done by the time you're 80?

Date:

*** Exercise 10: Goal setting ***

Take some time out of your busy schedule to think about some goals you would like to set for yourself.
These should be SMART

Specific - you can identify exactly what to do.

Measurable - you'll know when you've finished.

Achievable - you have or can get the resources.

Relevant - they are relevant to your larger goals.

Time - they have a time for completion.

	Short term goal	Date:
Today		
This week		
Next 30 days		

	Medium term goals	Date:
Two months time		
Three months time		

	Long term goals	Date:
1 year		
2 years		
5 years		

Assessments

Every module that you undertake at university will have some kind of assessment. Usually the first year's marks do not count towards your degree classification, so you can use this year to plan your studies well and have a practice at achieving high grades. This can then be assessed so that you can make a prediction about your degree classification.

So many students go through university or college without any time planning, goal setting or preparation for assessment and their marks suffer because of this.

Assessments will be in many different forms. You may be asked to complete an assignment, a case study, present some research, complete an in class test, present a portfolio or a formal examination. You must always remember that being at university is at a higher level than your school course which means you have to increase your efforts and skills to achieve high grades.

Assessment Criteria Explained

Every piece of work that you have to complete as part of your degree programme will have an assessment criteria. This is a set of statements that will categorise which classification your piece of work will be awarded. A member of the academic team decides on the assessment criteria when they write the module document.

This will usually be a grid with mark ranges relating to degree classification and the set of criteria needed to achieve that grade. Within the table will then be a set of statements that your assignments will fit into.

Following there is an example showing just some of the categories for the assessment criteria for a module.

It is important that you read the assessment criteria before you start your assignment as this will tell you exactly how this piece of work will be marked and you will be able to match your work to the criteria and probably guess what grade your tutor will award before you hand it in. This should be available online, or possibly in your course handbook, if not ask the departmental office for a copy. Tutors will rarely hand them out so you need to be active to find the information. This information will help you be strategic about how much time you spend on each assignment.

Sometimes it is a good idea to read your assignment out loud to someone who knows nothing about your subject. Then you will know if it reads correctly and you can also check if you have commas, full stops and paragraphs in all the right places. Another way is to get your fellow students to peer review your work so that they award it with a mark. [A peer is someone with a similar level of skills to you.]

Once you have received your mark back from your tutor you should be able to then reflect on the feedback and make some notes on how you may improve for the next time.

You may also wish to book an appointment with your module tutor to ask how you might improve your grade.

Reflection is important otherwise you will carry on making the same mistakes and receiving the same grade.

Make sure you use the time management tools to plan out your time to make sure you get your assignments done well ahead of time.

Assessment Grid

Module title	Psychology	Notes/marks
Module code	PY105	
Credits	30	
Module leader	John Smith	
My lecturers	Betty Brown Peter Pen	Mainly Dr Brown
Assessment	**Date**	
1 x 2000 word essay (35%)	15th Nov	62 % (21.7)
1 x 2 hour exam (35%)	10th Jan	42 % (14.7)
1 x 30 min group presentation (30%)	Week starting 3rd Dec	55 % (16.5)
	Overall mark	48%
Other: Assessment feedback Assignment feedback	 21st Jan 21st Jan	Feedback: On exam I didn't have time for question 4, which was worth 20% so Dr Brown was quite pleased with my knowledge but says I need to work on my time management in exams.

The numbers in the right hand column in brackets are the marks times the percentage for that assignment divided by 100 (eg. (62x35)/100 = 21.7). These will then add up to your overall module mark. Be warned, this may be out by 1-2 % from your actual recorded mark as the rounding may work differently in the official spreadsheet.

*** Exercise 11: Your module assessment grid ***

Complete an assessment grid for all your modules that you will study this year.
This will help you to become focused and organized.
Remember you can download more forms from www.uolearn.com

Module title		Notes/marks
Module code		
Credits		
Module leader		
My lecturers		
Assessment	**Date**	**Marks**
	Overall mark	
Other:		

Level 1: Developing Academic and Personal Skills Portfolio Assessment Criteria (partial table only, from 1 university, others will differ)

	I (70-79%)	Fail (39-26%)
Portfolio Tasks Completeness of the portfolio including appropriate coverage, focus and progression of specific tasks set	Excellent coverage of all of the tasks set, high level of synthesis of material with good progression, good focus on the material presented.	Basic coverage of the some of the tasks set but the file is incomplete, limited synthesis of material with little appropriate evidence of progression, limited focus on the material presented.
Research Skills Evidence of appropriate research skills to approach both familiar and unfamiliar situations	Evidence within the portfolio demonstrates a high level of research skills.	Evidence within the portfolio demonstrates a limited level of research skills.
Key and Transferable Skills Evidence of appropriate key and transferable skills including communication, numeracy, ICT and problem solving	Evidence within the portfolio demonstrates a high level of key and transferable skills.	Evidence within the portfolio demonstrates a limited level of key and transferable skills.
General Appropriate format, appropriate writing style, conciseness, grammar and sentence structure. Format and layout of portfolio	Presentation, sentence structure, grammar and spelling are wholly acceptable, clear and coherent writing style, clear and concise structure that was easy to follow, high level of comprehensibility	Presentation, sentence structure, grammar and spelling are below an acceptable standard, negligible evidence of an appropriate writing style little discernible structure, a largely inappropriate level of comprehensibility.

Assessment feedback

Lecturers spend hours and hours marking, writing or typing up feedback, so it is important when you receive your feedback or marks that you book an appointment with the tutor so that you can discuss the feedback for next time you write. You will increase your grades by reflecting on your feedback. Ask advice from your tutors to identify where you could have improved and if you were to carry out a piece of work next time what would be the best advice to increase the grade.

*** Exercise 12: Assignment Feedback ***

As part of your development collect all your assignment feedback sheets and look at the common themes that your tutors are saying about your assignments. Make a list of the common themes, these may be negative/constructive as well as positive e.g. not enough references, excellent referencing, good structure, poor layout, not enough reading, too much material. If you need help you may be able to book an appointment with a study advisor.

Advice on improvement	What did I do right?

Taking Effective Lecture Notes

It is important for you to turn up to your lecture well prepared. Make sure you have with you a pen, pencil and paper, ipad or other tablet to take notes. To make really useful notes a range of colored pens is a good idea as you can then color code different aspects of the lecture. The best ones are the highlighter and fineliner pens. Your lecturer may allow you to take in your lap top or smart phone so that you can take notes directly onto them.

It is a good idea to always write down the main title of the lecture and the date. This will help you to identify your notes later.

It is important that you listen carefully to what is being said so that you can pick out the points that will be key for you to remember. Don't try to write everything down that is being presented as before you know it the lecturer is on to the next slide and you are mid-sentence missing the main point. You could try learning speed writing (try speed writing by Heather Baker, www.uolearn.com).

Sometimes the notes will be posted on the university's intranet or VLE (virtual learning environment) before the lecture. Always make sure you're prepared and have downloaded your own copy. This means you can read about the lecture before it takes place and also make notes alongside what is being said. Notes should be taken in every lecture whether the lecturer provides hand-outs or not. Your own thoughts on the material will help you to understand the work much better than the printed hand-outs.

In terms of both understanding and remembering the lecture it is important to make connections with the rest of the information you have in your brain. A good lecturer will help you do this with examples and stories of how the information can be used but you must always be alert and make your own connections. The best way to do this is to set yourself questions that help flag up important points as you listen.

Before the lecture

Briefly remind yourself of any connecting lectures by looking through your previous notes or hand outs. Download and read any lecture notes that have been provided. Set yourself a specific question that you need answering about the probable content of the upcoming lecture. Write this under the title of the lecture.

During the lecture:

➢ Listen for the answer to your specific question.

➢ What's the story behind the theory?

➢ How does this lecture connect to your previous studies?

➢ How could you use the information being given?

➢ Is any of it relevant to possible exam questions?

➢ How could it be applied to a different situation?

➢ Which idea is the lecturer emphasizing?

➢ What 5 key words would summarize the lecture?

➢ Can you draw an image of what the lecture means to you?

In your notes use a different color for important points, specific quotes or formulae. Develop your own color coding system to use in all your lectures.

If you don't understand something ask straight away, if possible, and if not ask either the lecturer or your friends at the end. One principle that the best students have is they don't leave until they understand everything.

One of the best ways to take notes in lecture is through drawing yourself a concept map, mindmap or spider diagram (see the following pages). You can download free mindmapping software and aps quite easily.

After the lecture:

➤ Re-read your notes and add to them within 24 hours of the session.

➤ If there are still points you don't understand then follow them up on the internet, library, with friends or write them down as questions to ask when you have a tutorial.

➤ File your notes away systematically so that you can easily find them.

➤ Make sure you follow up on any suggested reading.

➤ Practice using any practical information like analysis techniques before the next lecture so that you can check you've understood them.

➤ Each week look through the previous week's notes.

An example of a mindmap:
(See www.uolearn.com to see it in detail and color.)

An example of a concept map:

Similar concepts are shown using the same shapes or colors and more detail is usually given than a mindmap.

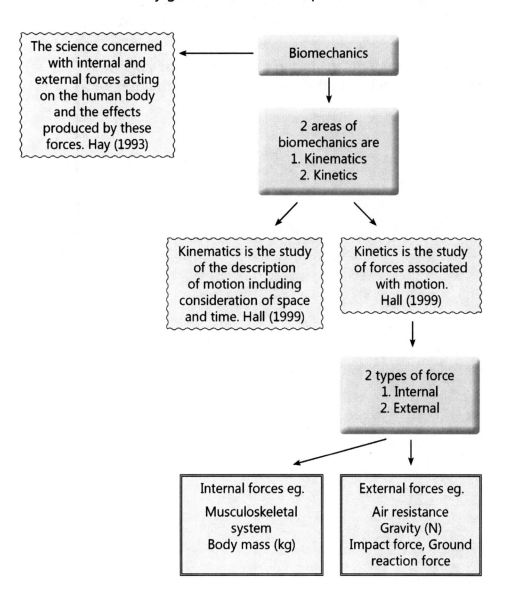

*** Exercise 13: Mind and Concept Mapping ***

Using a set of lecture notes produce a mindmap or concept map relevant to your studies. Choose any topic from any lecture. You may want to use this when you come to revise for your final exams.

I always advise students to start in the center of the page with the title of the lecture and then work outwards with notes and ideas.

Essay Planning and Writing

Do you have anxieties about writing? By the end of this section you will be able to stop your mind from becoming empty and know where to begin with your essay or project.

So how do you do all this?

✓ Firstly you need to clarify the task before you start researching, know what you are looking for, by examining the title and course notes really carefully. Find out exactly what is required; ask your tutor early on if you are unsure.

✓ Write one line to sum up your basic opinion or argument. Adapt it as you proceed.

✓ Produce a mindmap or a concept map to record what you know.

✓ Decide what you need to read or find out.

✓ Collect and record information.

✓ Get the information you need but be focused, be selective- you can't use everything.

✓ Write a set of questions to guide your research and look for the answers.

✓ Check the word limit to see how much information you can use for each point, and keep a notebook nearby to jot down all your ideas.

✓ As you go through your research keep on asking yourself, do I need this information, and if so how will I use it.

✓ You need to record information as you go along stating where you found the information and ideas for your reference list.

✓ Make a note of themes, theories, dates, data, names, explanations, examples, details, evidence and page numbers, as you go along as you will find it difficult to do this at the end of your essay.

When you have gathered the information, think about what you have discovered.

➢ Has your viewpoint changed?

➢ Have you clarified your argument?

➢ Have you enough evidence /examples?

➢ What arguments or evidences oppose your point of view?

➢ Are they valid?

➢ Is it clearer to you why this task was set?

When you are writing your outline plan and first draft you need to work out the order to introduce your ideas, using your mindmap, concept map or headings and points. Work out how many words you can write on each point, and don't be frightened of writing your first draft, start with whatever seems the easiest, just keep on writing, you will soon get into the flow. Don't worry about the style of your writing for now. To begin with just clearly state things and use simple short sentences.

Write out the title on a piece of paper in large handwriting so that you stay focused on the title when you are writing, so many students go off on a tangent and don't end up answering the question.

Underline the key words you are being asked to write about, describe, analyze, compare, contrast, explain etc.

Make sure that you leave time after writing the essay for editing (checking your work is concise and answers the question) and proofreading (checking for typos).

Verbs used in assignment titles

Verb	Interpretation
Account for	Explain why something happened
Account of	Describe the order in which events happened
Analyze	Break the topic down into smaller parts and show how they relate to each other, look for patterns
Assess	Consider all aspects that contribute, positive and negative, and then decide how important it was
Compare	Take 2 or more components and write about the same aspect for each one to find out what they have in common and how they differ.
Contrast	Same as compare but concentrate more on the differences.
Define	List the aspects which make that issue unique from all others, explain what it means.
Describe	Give the relevant attributes of the issue, if physical it would be size, color etc. if an event it could be the date, location, people involved etc.
Discuss	Debate the pros and cons of a situation
Evaluate	Same as assess
Explain	Give the reasons behind a situation, the causes and effects
To what extent, How far	Similar to assess but usually implies the reason given isn't the whole issue and is looking to you to give other explanations and weigh up which is the biggest influence.
Illustrate	Give specific examples
List	Similar to describe
Relate	Same as compare
Review	Go over the background and pull together various sources to give a single picture
State	Similar to describe
Summarize	Give the major points

These are only guidelines, the actual wording of your question will determine your approach.

Case Study: Learning to write

In the first six weeks of starting university Julian was asked to write a 1,000 word assignment which had to be submitted using the correct layout for the assignment. It had to include referencing from at least four books, three journal articles, a government report or policy, two newspapers and three relevant websites. This was quite a daunting task for Julian as he had never written in the third person before. He was used to writing descriptively using the words 'I think this because of that'. Now he had to start to learn how to write more academically using the words 'Various studies suggest that'. This was difficult for Julian at first but he learnt how to progress with his skills by having regular appointments with his personal tutor and asking for feedback. The most important skill that he learnt was that reading was the key to writing. The more he read the more he understood how the academics wrote their articles and so he adopted the same style.

Structure of an Essay

> **Introduction**

In your introduction refer directly to the title and in order to focus your reader, say how you interpret the title. You can do this by rephrasing the title in your own words

> **Main body**

In this section you need to present the arguments and evidence for and against the proposed theory. You need to make sure that you evaluate not only the main theory but also mention any competing ideas and why they are not convincing. You need to give the arguments for and against each issue. All of the evidence you present must be referenced to creditable sources.

> **Conclusion**

Refer back to your question to demonstrate to your reader that you are still answering the set question contained in the title and summarize what you have written about.

> **Final draft**

Read it aloud to check that it is clearly written. Keep on re-drafting until you are happy with the text. Get somebody independent to read through and look for spelling mistakes and to tell you if it doesn't read well.

Sometimes your tutors will allow you to book an appointment to discuss your first draft of your assignment. It is not a good idea to go and see your tutor the day before it is due to be handed in. Plan your time appropriately to complete your draft.

When you have received feedback you can then start to write up your final copy.

Remember your word count. You will lose marks for being under or over, there is usually a 10% leeway. Make sure you stay within this as some tutors fail your assignment if it is under or over.

Giving a Presentation

Giving a presentation can be nerve wracking but doesn't need to be. The main thing is that you need to prepare both your content and yourself before you start. Even though you may only be giving a short presentation, be professional about it.

Preparing your content:

✓ Use the key points.
✓ Keep your visual aids simple and very large font (30 point on PowerPoint)
✓ Remember they are not to help you; they are to help the audience understand
✓ Use bullet points
✓ Have no more than 1 slide per minute (and preferably less)
✓ Practice the talk to check the length
✓ Have a clear introduction, middle and if possible end with a summary of the three main points
✓ Use pictures as well as words on your slides. You may also import video or audio clips which makes the presentation more interesting.
✓ Use any animation functions sparingly - it's about the content
✓ Have a reference list on your final slide.

Prezi.com is a really useful presentation tool that can be shared on the web. This is becoming a more popular way to present with an easy to use interface.

Preparing yourself:

✓ Dress a little smarter than usual
✓ Check out what equipment will be available in the room
✓ Make hand outs for your audience (so they can listen to you)
✓ Breathe deeply to calm yourself
✓ Before you start, think of anything that you are confident at (it doesn't have to have any connection with the presentation it will just give you confident body language)
✓ Stand tall.
✓ Look at your audience (tip if you're using a computer or an overhead projector then look at them not the screen behind you)
✓ Don't cross your arms
✓ Don't read from your notes.

*** Exercise 14: Questions and checklist for a presentation. Before a presentation use this to help plan. ***

Title of talk	
Date of presentation	
Time	
Length	
Location	
Who are the audience? age/gender/background	
How many will there be?	
What do they know about the topic?	
What do they need to know? Why do they need the information?	
What don't they need to know?	
What questions might they ask?	
Can I get the audience to participate?	
What equipment is in the room?	
How will the room be laid out? (rows/groups)	
What audio/visual aids should I use? What's my backup plan?	
Are there any health and safety issues?	

Writing a Scientific Lab Report

If you are studying a scientific programme at university then you will carry out some practicals and maybe expected to analyze the results. From this analysis you may, as part of your assessment, have to write a lab report. There should be a set of guidelines provided on how the department wants you to write the report. This will probably be found in the course or module booklet.

The aim of any report is to communicate efficiently and provide sufficient (but not excessive) detail so that others could replicate the study described. It is also for the lecturer to see that you carried out the experiment correctly.

The simple rule for lab reports is that they must be written in the third person, past tense. Never use any names or I, me, we, she, he.

Prepare yourself before you go into the lab by getting all your equipment in one place and reading the method script. Look carefully at the timing and the order of the steps. When you are in the lab, make sure you make a table to put the information in. It is best to get a separate notebook to keep all your results in as bits of paper are easily lost. If you have to make a graph in the lab make it neat and tidy, then you may be able to use it in your report without redrawing it.

The format for a lab report should be:

➢ **Title**
The title should be placed on the head of the report and should be as brief as possible. The title should also reflect the nature of the study, eg. Reaction time as a function of practice. Try to avoid the use of phrases such as 'experiment to show'.

➢ **Abstract**
This should be summarized as briefly as possible in a single paragraph, stating what was done, why and give information about the method and the participants. Tell the reader what was found and state whether the findings were expected or unexpected. You will need to state whether the differences were significant or not (if statistical analysis has been conducted).

➤ Introduction

An introduction gives some background about the topic under investigation and includes reference to published work. You must give a reason or reasons for the study, stating which hypothesis is being tested. This should set the scene.
It may include a literature review if appropriate.

➤ Method

The method should contain a number of subsections.

- **Participants**

  If you have undertaken an experiment where you have taken measurements on people (eg. speed of running in sports or blood pressure in biology) then you need to give relevant details such as age, experience and gender.

- **Research design:**
  What research methods have you used and why?

  Describe exactly what happened in the study. Provide sufficient detail and clarity so that a reader unfamiliar with the study could copy it, given the same type of subjects and equipment. Make sure that you rewrite the method in your own words and include any variations you made.

- **Analytical technique:**

  Describe any analytical techniques that you will apply to the data; justifying why they were chosen.

➤ Results

The results should give a brief description of the data and then the analysis of it. You should present your analysis as tables and graphs which must have titles and labels.

State what statistical test or equation was applied to the data and report the results of the test. No discussion of the analysis should be written about in this section, this is merely a statement of the main findings of the study.

➤ Discussion

You must relate the findings to the hypothesis described in the introduction, and then discuss the findings in relation to previous work. State what further questions are raised by the experiment and what the limitations were.

➢ Conclusion

Summarize your research and state what you would do differently if you were to carry out the experiment again.

➢ References

You need to add a list of any books, articles or internet sites that you have used to help write the report. This should be done using the Harvard referencing system (see later). You may also need to include a literature review.

The most common things that you should check for are:

➢ That the abstract does not contain trivial details which are not of central importance.

➢ That the findings are summarized, whether statistically significant or not.

➢ That there is not too much background information in the introduction.

➢ That there is sufficient rationale for the study.

➢ That your writing does not include the names of the experimenters or personal pronouns such as I, we, he, she.

Thinking Critically

When you are asked to write about the most important aspects of a theory, issue, argument etc. you will automatically need to think about the arguments for and against. You need to comment on each argument and decide which you agree with and why. This is critical thinking.

Critically doesn't mean make negative comments, it means you should question the information and compare it to other available information.

You need to think of it like being a detective; you need to investigate and check all claims that are being made by everyone involved in the chain of events. This includes your own lecturers and any material you might read. If someone claims a hypothesis is true you need to compare it to the evidence they have provided. Often there may even be conflicting claims based on the same evidence. Who is right, one of them, both or neither? Is the logic sound as they've moved from step to step? It's your job to solve the mystery.

Analytical Thinking

- ✓ Be objective
- ✓ Examine every aspect of an issue
- ✓ Check the evidence
- ✓ Look for flaws
- ✓ Compare it to other theories
- ✓ Contrast it with other theories
- ✓ Show you understand why people reach certain conclusions
- ✓ Show which arguments and theories you agree with and why (without the use of I)
- ✓ Use the correct academic language

Critical Questions

- ➢ Who?
- ➢ What?
- ➢ Why?
- ➢ When?
- ➢ Where?
- ➢ How?

Reading Critically

When you start to read for your degree you need to start asking questions in your mind - become the detective

- ➢ Is the evidence reliable?
- ➢ How reliable is the content of the article?
- ➢ Is it from a refereed journal? Have the journal articles that you have chosen been peer reviewed so that they have been read and approved by practitioners and professionals in that field?
- ➢ What is the author saying (the abstract and conclusion will give an indication of this)?
- ➢ What do you want to get from the article?
- ➢ Is there enough detail so that I fully understand this? Or do I need to do more background reading?
- ➢ Are there any problems with the methodology that the author has used to gather their evidence?
- ➢ Does the evidence provided by the author fully support the arguments put forward or the conclusions drawn?
- ➢ How can I use the understanding gained from this article in a wider context (eg. relate it to other aspects of the course/ other modules)?

Always look at the reading materials your lecturers have recommended on the reading lists. These are generally the books or journal articles your tutors want you to use for your assignments. At the end of every lecture the lecturer should provide information on where their reading came from so it is worth making a note of this, as this will give you reading materials for your assessments.

Make sure when using internet sources that they come from reliable sites, otherwise you may lose marks. It is better to use books and journals as the main reading materials for your projects and assignments.
Unless you are giving a short quote (a couple of sentences), correctly referenced, then don't copy the text straight into your work. Always re-word the material as work is often checked out through plagiarism software.

Writing Critically

New students always tend to start off their writing for their degree by writing descriptively, the more you develop on your degree programme and start to write analytically the more marks you will gain.

Here is an example of the differences:

Descriptive writing	Critical analysis
States what happened	Analyzes why something happened and its significance.
Describes what something is like	Evaluates strengths and weaknesses of something
Explains a theory	Weighs up a theory against others and relates theory to practice
States when something works	Investigates why something works or does not work, using examples and case studies
Identifies methods used	Explains why methods were used and investigates alternatives.
Lists things in order	Uses a logical structure with signposts and links, forms conclusions before moving on, reaches an overall conclusion

One of the ways to improve your writing is to read as many journal articles as possible on the given subject. Underline or highlight the first three or four words of every paragraph and highlight the key theme throughout the article. From this you will be able to use the beginning of the paragraph for your writing of your assignment and you will be able to use the key themes to back up your critical analysis.

Free Writing

In order for you to improve your writing skills it's important to be able to allow your writing to flow. As technology has taken over a large part of our lives the art of writing is becoming less popular and sentence structure and use of correct grammar is even less fluent.

In order for you to keep up the art of writing it's important that you regularly practice free writing.

Sit in a quiet place with a pen and notebook and start to write about the day's events noting down how you felt and observations that you made throughout the day. Just let your mind and the words flow. Even if your mind becomes blocked then write down the first word that comes into your mind and write around the word. With regular exercise of carrying out this task you will develop your art in writing. Story writing is also a way in which you can develop your imagination and creativity to introduce you to new words and to the concept of structure.

Read back out loud what you have written, soon you will be able to write around many different topics.

Keeping a daily journal is a great way to develop your writing style. Try and start a travel journal when you are on holiday writing about the day's events.

Good writers all started somewhere. Today it's your turn.

*** Exercise 15: Thinking critically ***

Find a research article relating to a recent course you've done.
Identify the key themes that are running through the article.
What arguments are being presented?
What evidence is there to support the arguments?
Does the article reach a conclusion?
Do you think the arguments support the conclusion?

Referencing

In order for you to complete your assignments you will need to know how to reference correctly. You will lose marks if you do not reference correctly. Referencing is often referred to as citing and means taking ideas or words from something you have read, listened to or watched and putting them into your assignment to support your discussion or analysis. Whenever you use the work of someone else in your coursework, you must reference the source in your assignment text and in your bibliography or reference list.

A reference list is all the references you have referred to in your assignment/project/essay.
A bibliography is a list of all the works that you have read that contributed to your thinking process but that you haven't referenced directly in your writing.
If you reference correctly, your tutors will be able to check your sources for accuracy and you will avoid plagiarism.

Plagiarism means taking somebody's ideas, words or inventions and using them as your own without referencing the source. More commonly now students are cutting and pasting documents from the internet without referencing the source. This means is that when the lecturers submit an electronic copy of your work through plagiarism software it will pick up exactly where the work has come from.

When referencing work, the style that you use in the reference list or bibliography is different from the way that you reference in your text in your assignments. Over the many years that I have been teaching, I always get my first year undergraduate student to complete a simple exercise that will allow them to understand referencing within a text and in a bibliography. Once you have completed this task you will then be able to refer back to the template when you are writing your assignments and gain marks for your referencing style. Here is an example:

Book single author text:
In the text you give the author's name and date of the text only e.g. Hepworth (2011)
In your reference list at the end it would look like this:
Hepworth, A., (2011). Studying for your Future. Lancashire. Universe of Learning Ltd.

The best system to use is the Harvard system as your lecturers will understand it and think it to be the professional way to treat references.

For a really good guide to referencing visit http://libweb.anglia.ac.uk/referencing/harvard.htm

Book references:
An example from the Harvard system for a book, author, (date) published, title, location of publishers, publishers name.

Baker, H., (2010). *Speed Writing Skills Training Course*, Lancashire, Universe of Learning

Then if you referred to the book in the text you'd put (Baker, 2010).

Journal references
author names, date, article title, journal, volume number, (part number), page number.
This time you'd put the journal name in italics not the article title.

Greenhall, M.H., Lukes, P.J., Petty, M.C. Yarwood, J. and Lvov,Y., 1994. The formation and characterization of Langmuir-Blodgett films of dipalmitoylphosphatidic acid. *Thin Solid Films* 243 (1-2), pp.596-601

Web references:
In the Harvard system you'd put author, date, page title, web address, [date accessed].

Baker, H, (2009), *10 uses for speed writing*, http://www.uolearn. com/speedwriting/10usesofspeedwriting.html, [Date accessed 30/06/11]

*** Exercise 16: Harvard referencing ***

Find examples of the following types of information sources for your course and write out the references in the Harvard system, saying both how it would look in the text and in the reference section.

Information	Referencing
Book with multiple authors	In text: In reference:
Secondary citation	In text: In reference:
Contribution in an edited book	In text: In reference:
Ebook	In text: In reference:
Electronic journal	In text: In reference:
Blog	In text: In reference:
Official publication or government report	In text: In reference:

Information	Referencing
Act of parliament	In text: In reference:
Thesis	In text: In reference:
Newspaper	In text: In reference:
Television or radio programme	In text: In reference:
Film	In text: In reference:
Video/dvd	In text: In reference:
Music CD	In text: In reference:
Email	In text: In reference:

*** Exercise 17: Referencing List ***

Provide a referencing list for one of your assignments. Again, your tutor can look at this to see what aspects you are not getting quite right or to praise you as you have managed to grasp how to reference very early on in your course. Choose a variety of sources such as books, journals, websites to show examples of each type of reference.

Your reference list should be in alphabetical order of the first author's surname. For sources without named authors such as websites they should be listed in alphabetical order of the title.

Case study: Using referencing

Once Harvard referencing had been mastered, Sarah found that her assignments looked more professional in their presentation. This helped her to gain more marks as her tutors could see that she had carried out research for the assignment. Sarah used lots of books and journals for her assignments as her tutors emphasized that some websites may not be reliable and that books and journals provided a better resource. Also, the tutors were more familiar with the reading materials Sarah had used. Sarah also realized that it was important that she included a substantial number of resources in the bibliography and referencing list related to the word count of the assignment, for example if her assignments were 3,000 words she used no less than ten references. Sarah says that this is what she feels helped her to achieve her high grades.

How to carry out a Literature Review

A literature review is an overview of other people's work. The purpose may be to get you to understand the data better, in which case your writing will be descriptive and be a summary of the resources (like a huge abstract covering all the sources). However, the purpose may be for you to combine the sources and synthesis a composite view of all the ideas. Get clarification from your tutor about exactly which type they are expecting. You need to find or research the most relevant comments, materials, studies, reviews, articles and chapters that support your study.

Types of sources:

➤ **Primary source** - this is the actual evidence, examples could be an account from that period in history, a research paper where the authors did the research themselves, a painting from the time of the event, a film, a photo etc.
➤ **Secondary sources** - where someone is commenting on a primary source or has reviewed range of primary sources.
➤ **Tertiary source** - where the main content is drawn from other summary documents. So perhaps the author has read only reviews and not used the primary sources themselves.

You need to identify which type of source your tutor is expecting you to use. Do they want you to read books (often tertiary sources) or the sources closer to the real data such as the papers written by people who either carried out the work or have seen the primary sources?

To assess how close your chosen resource is to the primary source look at their reference list, if the main references are reviews and books then your author may be quite distant from the original data and be only interpreting other people's work (similar to your own review).

You also need to get a feel for how many sources your tutor wants you to use. It is best to narrow down your research as much as possible; you don't want to read thousands of papers.

You need to largely stick with papers and books not random internet sources. The reason is that books have editors who check the content and papers are refereed by other experts in the area before they are allowed to be published. This doesn't always mean they are correct; just that the reviewers believed that the evidence and arguments presented were logical and fitted with the body of knowledge known up to that point.

It can often help to start with someone else's literature review on the same topic. Just put your topic and the word review into your search box. Usually you want to use specialist databases of papers not normal search engines. Ask your librarian for passwords.

How to carry out a literature review

- ✓ Make an action plan to make sure you have enough time for each part
- ✓ Write out a summary statement of up to 3 sentences of what the review will be about
- ✓ Ask staff for their expertise in recommending reading materials
- ✓ Look at your recommended reading on your programme booklet
- ✓ Find out who the key researchers are in your area of research and read around other work they may have done
- ✓ Do computer searches, as an academic you need to try and avoid sites that are not reliable
- ✓ Read, read, read and record: full references, hypothesis, subjects, methodology, statistics, findings, future studies/research, limitations of the study, any other key references
- ✓ Group similar references together
- ✓ Look for key themes emerging
- ✓ If your references agree then the synthesis is easier
- ✓ If you find conflicting arguments you may need to look for later review articles which help to understand the differing points of view.
- ✓ Once you've read all your material make a plan for writing, a mindmap, concept map or flow chart are great ways of getting an overview
- ✓ Always stay focused, keep your research question in mind

Reading your sources

- ➢ Collect your sources
- ➢ Write down around three questions you need to answer
- ➢ Look at every page for two seconds
- ➢ Evaluate the references (How useful will they be and how easy to read?)
- ➢ Prioritize them in order of importance
- ➢ Leave it one for two days (this lets your mind organize the data).
- ➢ For each reading source read the abstract or a short summary, then again look at each page for two seconds. Then read in the order that makes most sense to you. You don't need to read everything.

For more advice on reading get a book on speed reading.

It may be a good idea to buy some file cards and note down the name of the book, year, author, publisher, place of publishing and quotes you could use. On the other side, write a summary of the source.

If you keep all your file cards in a record box you will always have a record for your bibliography. There is software that helps you to track your references, some common ones are Refworks, Zotero and Endnote. Ask your librarian whether your university has installed any referencing software and you can store all your assignment references in one place. Alternatively you could use excel or any other spreadsheet/database programme to store the data.

University libraries subscribe to most journals electronically now and you can access them for free, just ask for a password at the library. If you find a book, that your library doesn't stock, you can request it via interlibrary loan. Interlibrary loans can take a while to arrive and there may be a charge.

Writing the review

➢ Look at the section on essay writing and critical writing again
➢ Have an introduction explaining why the review is being done and what sort of sources you've used, explain the structure of your review
➢ The main part should have some logical order, this depends on the content of your review but some options are:
  • By chronological order of the information
  • By chronological order of the sources
  • By trend, a section for each new idea and links as to how they led into each other
  • By research group (particularly for scientific reviews)
  • By major ideas or themes
  • By geographical location
➢ The summary should bring together the arguments and perhaps include questions to consider that arise from the material (particularly if the purpose is to start a dissertation or research project)

➢ Include varied but relevant primary sources and synthesize them well into the context of your study.
➢ Show evidence of extensive research particularly primary sources.
➢ Divide your review into sections and subheadings to give it a clear structure.
➢ Focus the literature review towards the direction of your study, link in importance of your study.
➢ Critically evaluate the literature and discuss it (using the third person)
➢ Include clearly identified, focused research questions at the end.

Preparing for your Exams

Once you know the dates for your examinations it will take some planning to get yourself ready for the date. Many students make the common mistake of leaving everything to the last minute.

✓ The first thing that you need to do is to organize your notes to find out what you do know and what you don't

✓ Reduce your notes to key headings, points and references

✓ Produce a mindmap of all you have to revise

✓ Print off lecture notes from either student folders, your virtual learning environment or files that the university have provided for you

✓ Print off past papers, sometimes there is still work left on the system from the year before so you can access last years examination questions to help you revise for this year's subjects

Passing an exam starts in your lectures and seminars:

At the end of lecture notes or during lectures there may be task questions. These might give some indication of what will be on your examination paper.

Make sure you understand how many marks will be required for you to pass your exam. It is also important for you to understand the marking of each question, for instance if there is a question that is worth 6 marks, make sure you write down six points or three lots of in depth answers so that you will be awarded two marks for each relevant point.

It is really important to attend all of your lectures, it is well researched that the students who turn up for lectures obtain the greatest marks. You can't understand all the relevant points made in a lecture from a Powerpoint presentation, you have to engage in discussion and listen in the lecture to the questions that are being asked.

Often in your lectures at exam time your lecturers will direct you indiscreetly to areas of importance for revision. Always remember it is in the key interest of a lecturer to teach you to pass your exams, not to have to fail you.

When looking at formulas in lectures and seminars, remember them for your exams, as these will not usually be written down for you.

Work out the answers to a range of possible exam questions for each topic, so that you feel able to deal with almost any question that might be set in the topics you have chosen.

Draw up a timetable for your exams, which will require you to work out exactly how much time you have to revise. Don't leave it to the last minute. At least four weeks before your exam begin to put together your revision notes. The pitfalls of revision include leaving revision to the last minute and finding ways of putting off revision (such as urgent things that need to be done i.e. watching television and socializing).

Making revision notes

Some people think that just by working hard and repetition that the material will stick so they follow strategies like:

* Reading through notes over and over again
* Writing notes out over and over again
* Writing out essays and learning them off by heart

These can help but it is much better to engage in actively reorganizing the data.

- ✓ Condense your notes or mindmap them
- ✓ Use color for different concepts
- ✓ Make flash cards of the key points
- ✓ Read your notes out aloud
- ✓ Meet with someone else and discuss likely exam questions
- ✓ Practice previous exam questions from past papers

It may also be a good idea when you are reading your journal and books for revision, as well as writing assignments for exams, to make a note on file cards of the title of the book, the year the book was written, the place the book was published and the publisher's name. On the opposite side of the card you can note down key themes and quotes that you want to use from the book. This way the book can go back to the library and you have a copy of everything you require from that resource.

Another good way to organize your notes is to color code your notes either into subjects or a traffic light system whereby you use green, red and yellow to distinguish what you have read, what you need to read and what you can put to one side to read over again and again. This will help to keep you organized and keep your notes distinguished.

Memory

You will need to use your memory effectively when you are revising and one way to do this is to read your notes after the lecture, a day after the lecture and a week after the lecture. Once you come to revise for your exams you will be able to read over the notes again and then put them into the colored category that means you understand and memorize what has been written on that certain part of the subject. This timing has been scientifically proved to be the best way to memorize complex facts.

In your working memory you only have space for 7 items at once so when you're revising it its best to stick to just 4 ideas at once. That way you have space to make the connections to the rest of the information stored in your brain.

If you revise in bursts of 15 minutes, with a short 2 minute break, it helps to refocus your attention as most people's attention span is about 20 minutes.

Always give yourself a comfort break after one or two hours. Go and do something else, get bit of fresh air and drink a glass of water as this will help to rehydrate your brain.

What you need to take with you to your exam

- ❑ Pens (2 black/blue and 1 red, [if allowed])
- ❑ Eraser
- ❑ Pencil
- ❑ Sharpener
- ❑ Highlighter pen
- ❑ Ruler
- ❑ Calculator
- ❑ Any open book materials that you are allowed
- ❑ Bottle of Water
- ❑ Student ID card and number

During the exam

- ✓ Start by reading the instructions, the format of the exam may have changed even if it has been the same for 10 years
- ✓ Read all the questions carefully and allocate the time you have for each, allowing checking time at the end
- ✓ Choose which ones to attempt - it is usually best to start with the easiest as then you'll gain confidence and get in the flow
- ✓ Take your time when selecting the correct answer during multiple choice exams
- ✓ As soon as you get in write down formulas and details that you have remembered
- ✓ Read over your answers again at the end

> ***** Exercise 18: Exam preparation *****
>
> Draw up a revision timetable using your time management grid (exercise 8) to show where you will be able to fit in time for revision.

Degree Enrichment

It is really important that you utilize the time that you have away from the university, spending quality time progressing towards your chosen goals and dreams. This is so that an employer can look at your curriculum vitae and see that you have done work above and beyond what was expected of you at university.

Degree enrichment may involve the following:

- Volunteering to help out in a school
- Volunteering / working in a care home
- Working for an organization or charity fund raising
- Coaching a sport abroad
- Organizing events for children during the school holidays.
- Working in summer holiday camps where students are paid for working with young adults and children, particularly in America.
- Working with Voluntary Services Overseas, which is an organization that can give you the opportunity to work in third world countries making the lives of the poor people better using the skills that you have.
- Going into schools and listening to the children read.
- Contacting the local parish council to see if there are any schemes you can become involved in.
- Sports teams
- Positions of responsibility in your clubs and college
- Part time work

Case study: Volunteering

Jenny had already completed a first aid course as part of her work with the St. John Ambulance. She had worked at events before she came to University. Through her course she then completed a further first aid certificate. She offered her services as a first aider to the student union during their sports activities. This often meant travelling away with the teams to other universities.

Jenny was offered the opportunity to apply for a position working for the Red Cross, even though this was nothing to do with her degree programme. This set Jenny up with a graduate job, earning a good salary with the opportunity of travelling around the world to different countries, training with the British Red Cross.

Volunteering

Sometimes in life we have to be prepared to go the extra mile to get to where we want to be.

Through your goal setting one of the aims may be to gain experience in your chosen field. If there is no paid work available in those areas you may want to give up a couple of hours of your time every week or once a month to work shadow or volunteer.

There is statistical evidence to prove that employment positions are given to someone who is already doing the job.

You can volunteer for a few hours to demonstrate your enthusiasm. Once your foot is in the door you will be able to see what opportunities are available. The amount of time you're able to spend with a company maybe very small but it will be a great asset when you come to apply for other jobs and you will have specific examples you can use. There are specific websites you can log onto for volunteering opportunities.

There are lots of voluntary organizations which you can apply to, some volunteering opportunities are available overseas, but you might have to pay. It may be useful to contact your local place of worship to find out if they have any projects you could help out with abroad. The National Trust offers a lot of positions too.

It looks really impressive on your CV if you have been a volunteer at some point, even if it is just for a few events.

Reflecting over the years of being involved with students it has become apparent that the most successful students have always been the students who have been prepared to go and find their own opportunities. Some students whilst completing their undergraduate degree work part time to support their families, and also find time to take on a volunteering role as well at their local clubs helping children or the elderly. They often achieve high grades and a place on their next course of study or quickly get a great job in their chosen field.

By volunteering either in your own country or going abroad, it broadens your experience of working both independently and as a team member making a contribution to society which will give you a sense of worthiness.

*** Exercise 19: Volunteering ***

Make a list of volunteering opportunities you might like to become involved in. It may be towards your chosen career or it may be something that you aspire to carrying out eg. helping to build a school in Ghana.

Write a paragraph on each of the volunteering schemes that you have been involved with and say how you feel they benefitted you.

Notes:

Chapter 3:

Skills development for employability

"The people who get on in this world are the people who get up and look for the circumstances they want, and, if they can't find them, make them." George Bernard Shaw

Chapter 3:
Skills development
for employability

During the first year of university it takes a few weeks to settle back into studying and there is always the sociable aspect of university to become involved in, especially if it's your first time away from home. It is important that all the way through your years at university you start to develop the skills you are going to need to allow you to get through your degree programme and also be able to offer to future employers. Normally, it is the second year of university when students start to realize that if they really started to work hard at their degree then they could really achieve a high grade of degree classification. As well as working towards your degree, you have to start thinking 'outside the box' about employment, as it is during this year that you are laying the foundations for future employability.

The next sections will guide you through exactly what you need to be doing to prepare yourself for employment.

Once you start university it is important that you keep focusing on your goals and also spend time thinking about career prospects. Have a look now at the goals and dreams you have set for yourself in chapter 2. Do you have any new goals to add?

When you start your degree you may have a certain career in mind and it is quite common to change your mind as you go through your degree. It is also very common to get into your third year of your degree and still not know which career path you wish to follow. This section will help you to gain the skills required to be able to say to an employer 'I have this skill and this is how I have applied it' and also to help guide you onto the path of your chosen career.

Strengths Weaknesses Experiences Achievements Threats (SWEAT)

You may be asked at interview to carry out a SWEAT or SWOT analysis. The O is Opportunities that may be ahead of you.

➢ Strengths

Write a paragraph about what you are really good at doing. What do you feel confident about? For example are you confident at speaking to large groups of students, good at presentation skills or proficient at organizing meetings and large events. Five strengths would be sufficient.

➢ Weaknesses

Write a paragraph about what you feel lets you down about yourself from a personal perspective as well as from an academic perspective. This may include those skills that you are not good at that you need to improve upon. For example, not finishing things, poor time management, writing skills etc. Three of these will be sufficient.

➢ Experiences

Write a paragraph about the good experiences that have happened to you that have helped you to develop your skills. This may be experiences you might have gained whilst studying for your degree or other activities. For example passing your driving test, working in a team, a personal challenge such as a sponsored walk etc.

➢ Achievements

Write a paragraph about your achievements in the past twelve months. This can be through your work or maybe through a hobby. It could include becoming good at something, competing in a sporting event etc. We are often poor at celebrating our successes so dig deep and what you think isn't an achievement may be a huge achievement to someone else so write it down.

➢ Threats

Write a paragraph about what takes you out of your comfort zone. What do you feel is more challenging to you that you will have to work on? What makes you feel very uncomfortable before the event occurs, during the event or after the event? What could stop you achieving your goals: illness, other people, lack of resources, etc.?

*** Exercise 20: Carry out a SWEAT analysis for your coming year. ***

Strengths:

Weaknesses:

Experiences:

Achievements:

Threats:

Critical Analysis

At school you may have been asked to write quite descriptively. At university it is important that you increase your academic ability and learn to write at a higher level.

To enable you to write at this higher level you will be encouraged to read more books, journals etc. so that you can build up the resources you need to complete your assignments. Whilst you are reading through the materials you have chosen it is important to keep an open mind on the key themes and arguments that are being presented. We need to form an opinion as to which articles are supporting one side of the argument and find other articles that are going against the other's theories. Critical analysis is about presenting those findings, putting over the different points of view and writing in the third person (unless otherwise stated) that these are the conclusions that have been summarized.

If you look carefully at your assessment criteria that you get with your assignment brief, you will be able to see that often you need to master the skill of critical analysis to get the highest marks. Examples of assessment criteria could be:

Analysis and Interpretation

70% 1st Comprehensive coverage, focus and progression of the theoretical aspects. Precise and coherent evaluation of current guidelines of the uses of....

(60-69%) 2:1 Appropriate coverage of the theoretical aspects, good progression and focus. Largely appropriate evaluation of current guidelines.

(50-59%) 2:2 Reasonable coverage of the theoretical aspects and some appropriate focus and progression. Reasonable outline of evaluation of current guidelines but not fully explained.

(40-49%) 3rd Some coverage of the theoretical aspects but with little progression of focus. Basic evaluation of current guidelines that lacked clarity and were not fully explained.

<39% Fail Little coverage of the theoretical aspects illustrating little disciplinary knowledge. Largely inappropriate outline of evaluation of guidelines

*** Exercise 21: Critical analysis ***

Write about an issue on your degree programme, this can be about any subject.
Write about aspects of your chosen issue.

Use evidence to back up your arguments for or against.
Use examples to back up your argument
Reach a conclusion.

Problem Solving

With any task that you have to carry out whether it be in your personal or professional working life there maybe problems to solve. Some people bury their heads in the sand, wishing that the problem would go away and others tackle it head on like a bull in a china shop, when they could have spent some time evaluating their outcomes.

Worrying about a problem is a waste of good energy, you might as well use that energy to get the problem solved.

Let's look at a strategy for problem solving.

Firstly analyze your to do list for the day and identify if the problem is one of your priorities for the day. It might mean that if you solve this problem now or today it frees your mind up to deal with other issues.

"Don't put off till tomorrow what you can do today."

Sometimes when we have a lot to deal, with particularly when you are in a leadership or team situation, problems will build up until we feel that we can't deal with any of them and you may become overwhelmed. This can lead to breakdowns in communication, confusion over what task to do next and possibly even illness.

*** Exercise 22: Problem solving reflection ***

Write a reflective piece of writing about an incident or experience where you had to use problem solving skills to enable the incident or experience to have a positive outcome. If the experience that you are writing about didn't have a positive outcome state why and write about what you may do next time in that situation on reflection to change the situation from a negative to a positive outcome.

You may need to discuss your problem with somebody neutral to the situation. Ask them to listen to your point of view and add to your solution rather than criticise it.
Also, consider at this point what would happen if you didn't achieve the desired outcome. Would it be detrimental to your own health and well being?

*** Exercise 23: Problem solving ***

Identify a problem and write it down as a question.

....

....

Write a list of who it involves.

....

....

Write down the outcome you want to achieve from solving the problem.

....

....

....

Write a step by step list on how to tackle the problem.

....

....

....

....

....

....

Will you have to look at other alternatives or maybe a compromise?

....

For lots more problem solving questions see a list developed by the CIA http://bbh-labs.com/how-the-cia-define-problems-plan-solutions-the-phoenix-checklist

Motivating Others

In order to get through our everyday life we have to learn to have respect for others and how to get along with other people using different types of behavior patterns. We all soon learn what is acceptable behavior and what is not.

As part of your learning programme you will be grouped with peers. Some you will see as having acceptable behavior and some not. Yet, it will be out of your control to walk away. This may be because you may have a group presentation to put together or are working on a project where you've been assigned to groups.

Some people are born leaders in situations like this and some people will just sit back and let others do all the work.

The most common complaint of group work is that certain individuals have completed all the work and then others who hardly participated still gained a good mark as it was awarded to the group as a whole.

In order for individuals to be able to work together successfully the group has to become motivated.

Motivation levels will differ across the time of the planning of the presentation/projects depending on what other issues people have going on in their lives.

To keep others motivated it is important to have clear goals and a clear aim at the beginning of the procedure, to share the work load out equally and give everybody a time scale. If one leader cannot be agreed, have two for different parts of the project and instead of having a leader over the whole project have a coordinator who manages the two leaders. This way everybody will get clear and fair guidance on their roles in the team.

*** Exercise 24: Motivating others ***

At interview for a job you may be asked how you have actively motivated others.

Think about an event where you have had to motivate someone or a group of people to do something.

Think about the process, how did you achieve the desired outcome?

What skills did you use?

....

....

....

....

....

....

....

....

....

....

....

....

....

....

....

Effective Team Working

A team is composed of a number of individuals working towards a common goal. You may enjoy working on your own, working at your own pace, not being told by anyone what to do and organizing your work the way that you want it to be carried out. However, sometimes we work with other people to complete a task. A good exercise to have a look at is 'Belbin Team Roles', this will establish what role you usually play within a team, www.belbin.com. You may identify yourself as being the plant, the monitor evaluator, coordinator, resource investigator, implementer, completer finisher, team worker, shaper or specialist. A good team needs a mixture of these personalities and none are better than the others.

It is a really good idea to know how you operate in a team situation. One of the most important skills to make your team work effectively is communication.

Here are some ideas for effective team managers:

❑ Respect all of your team members.
❑ Make sure the team understands what is being asked of them.
❑ Make sure they know the project requirement thoroughly and know the project target is achievable and by when.
❑ Each member needs to have clearly defined roles and responsibilities to avoid confusion or overwork.
❑ Let everyone have their say.
❑ Listen to other people's opinions and use their suggestions but explain that if it doesn't work you'll try another way.
❑ Ask for feedback and suggestions.
❑ Give reasons for your actions.
❑ Praise your team.
❑ Avoid blaming others when work is not completed. Find out why it has not been completed and draw up a different strategy.
❑ Find out if one of the team members is facing any problems completing the work on time, find out the root cause and address the issue.
❑ Communication and approachability are very important.

Did you tick all the boxes? Then your team will have an excellent chance of working effectively.

As an effective team worker you may have to guide and support other team members and learn to understand the different behaviors and personalities and qualities that all team members bring to the group. Always stay focused on the goal and what ways the team can work best to achieve that goal.

*** Exercise 25: Effective team work ***

Questions may be asked about team work during job interviews so you need to have examples ready. Think about a situation where you have been part of a team.

What role did you play within the team?

Were you happy with your performance within that team?

How did the team stay motivated to carry out tasks together?

Did you have any problems carrying out your roles and if so how did you solve the problems that occurred?

....

....

....

....

....

....

....

....

....

....

....

Leadership Skills

Beyond the personal traits of a leader there are specific skills people must learn to master if they want to become a leader.

You must be an effective communicator to enable you to motivate people to work toward the group goal. You need excellent negotiation skills to help make sure everyone contributes their best to the project. You must be a good planner to be able to devise a plan to achieve the goal and then encourage people to complete the goal. Leaders must be realistic, polite but insistent, they constantly and consistently drive forward their goal.

"No goal is achievable unless you chip away at it every day." Ackah.

Do you regard yourself to be a good leader yes/no?

If not, what do you feel you need to improve to enable you to take on the leadership role?

➤ Believe in yourself more to increase your confidence?
➤ Greater clarity of your goals?
➤ Have a better knowledge of the skills and personalities of your group?

If you do regard yourself to be a good leader:

➤ What three words would you use to describe your leadership qualities?

Some examples may be motivational, inspirational, fair, direct, didactic ,approachable ,strong, versatile, proficient, organized, positive, competent and economical.

Again in an interview situation you may be asked to talk about or demonstrate how you have used your leadership qualities, providing examples.

*** Exercise 26: Leadership skills ***

What opportunities have you had to practice your leadership skills?

Can you plan any activities in the near future to give yourself more leadership skills?

Are there any leaders you admire?

How do they lead?

What do you think a good manager/leader needs to be able to do?

Can you find any books, particularly biographies of great leaders?

Case study: Working alongside your course

Julia attended university for three years and graduated with a 2:1 degree. She took an access course to get to university as she did not have the traditional entry requirements to enrol on her course.

Throughout her course there were opportunities to complete a work placement and work shadow health professionals as well as to take part time employed work at the weekends. Julia completed this whilst going through a break up of her marriage, losing her house and having nowhere to live with her family. She then worked as a volunteer for a company for six months, three hours per week offering her services in all the areas that the company provided.

Through this Julia was offered an excellent full time post with a very high starting salary upon graduating. Julia was delighted with this and she said

> *"You only get out of it, what you put in."*

Julia has now started a part time master's degree and is working towards a PhD so that she can get an even better job as her boys get older and less dependent upon her.

*** Exercise 27: What other skills do you have that will help you with your work? ***

We've talked about some skills that are useful in work and in study, what other skills do you have that an employer might be interested in?

....

....

....

....

....

Some ideas of skills you might have thought about:

Intellectual skills

You will also need to develop intellectual skills as part of your degree programme. These skills are associated with being able to demonstrate the initial ability to analyze, interpret and summarize data and information with guidance. You may be asked to substantiate arguments with a broad range of evidence.

Knowledge and understanding

You need to be able to demonstrate knowledge and understanding of the principles of your course and apply the principles to procedures using your tutor's guidance.

Practical skills

Your course may have an element of practical based skills and you will be able to build on this with experience. You must be prepared to take part in practicals if they are part of your course as this will help you to get the most out of your course.

Transferrable skills

Transferrable skills are skills you develop that can be used in many situations, examples include: communication, ICT skills, researching, practical investigations, leadership skills, time planning etc..

Effective learning and study skills

These also include effective reading, effective note taking, essay writing, revision skills, time management and managing your own learning. You will develop a range of oral and visual presentation skills. Research and written communication will be developed and enhanced whilst you're at university.

Independent learning

Independent learning strategies will be encouraged to supplement tutor delivered activities and other specific learning activities. You may also be asked to carry out computer based learning, class exercises, poster work and follow up project work following fieldwork or placement out in industry. As you get into your final year of your degree programme you will become involved in dissertation research which is a really large study. This will include planning, execution and completion and report production. Reading is the key to success on your degree programme.

Chapter 4:

Focusing on your career goals

"Often people attempt to live their lives backwards: they try to have more things, or more money, in order to do more of what they want so that they will be happier. The way it actually works is the reverse. You must first be who you really are, then, do what you need to do, in order to have what you want." Margaret Young

Chapter 4:
Focusing on
your career goals

Career Searches

It may be a good idea to book an appointment with your careers advisor whilst you are at university as it is a free service. Some universities extend their service for one year after you have left the institution to help you to start along your career path. Some students still don't know what they want to do. Other students think they know right from the start what they want to do and as they progress on their degree they change their minds. Visit your careers department early on as they have lots of great resources.

Through the use of goal setting you can devise a plan of where you see yourself and potential earnings. Often students say to me "I really don't know what I would like to do when I leave university." I've developed a series of questions to help them think about the type of environment and roles they see for themselves. Have a go, you can choose more than one option!

*** Exercise 28: Career forecast ***

1. What environment do you see yourself working in?

❑ Indoors	❑ Self employed
❑ Outdoors	❑ Public sector
❑ Office environment	❑ Big corporate
❑ Factory	❑ Small company
❑ Field	❑ Charity
❑ Lab	❑ Travelling around locally
❑ Forest	❑ Travelling nationally
❑ Beach	❑ Travelling the world
❑ Hospital	❑ Confined to one place
❑ School	❑ At a desk
❑ University	❑ Doing a physical job

Other ....

2. When in the day do you want to work?

- ❑ Daytime only
- ❑ Days and evenings
- ❑ Nights
- ❑ Shift work - mixed times
- ❑ Weekends
- ❑ Don't mind

3. What type of people do you want to work with?

- ❑ Children
- ❑ Young adults
- ❑ Prefer to work alone
- ❑ Adults only
- ❑ Elderly
- ❑ Mixed
- ❑ Special needs
- ❑ Don't mind

4. What interests you?

....
....
....
....
....
....

5. What salary do you want to be potentially earning in 5 years time?

....

6. What salary do you potentially want to be earning in 10 years time?

....

7. How many years do you want to stay in your job?

....

8. Where do you see yourself in 10 years time? This could involve a house, family, moving abroad moving into a managerial role etc. Where would you like to be living and what sort of house?

....

....

....

....

....

....

9. What salary is your absolute minimum you can work for to allow you to live and possibly pay back your student loan.

....

....

10. What salary do you want to be earning to live a comfortable lifestyle?

....

....

After answering those ten questions we can start to get an idea of the areas you would like to work in and from this you can establish whether you will need further training or are there already the jobs out there to match your skills.

Following is a list of job websites you can start to have a look at. Step out of your comfort zone as there is a big world out there and you may want to consider working abroad for a short time which could possibly end up long term or via a promotion back to this country.

List of websites to look for jobs

UK:

www.jobsite.co.uk (job centers)	www.jobs.ac.uk (universities)
www.hays.co.uk	www.whatjobsite.com/
www.totaljobs.com	jobs.guardian.co.uk
www.monster.co,uk	www.reed.co.uk
www.jobrapido.co.uk	www.office-angels.com
www.fish4.co.uk/jobs	www.pertemps.co.uk

US:

www.monster.com	www.careerbuilder.com
www.indeed.com	www.simplyhired.com
www.glassdoor.com	www.jobs.aol.com
www.usajobs.gov	www.snagajob.com
www.job.com	www.beyond.com

There will be specific jobsites for subjects that you are interested in. eg. sport related websites, jobs specific to nursing etc. The best place to find jobs is in the specialist magazines for your chosen area, eg. New Scientist, Times Educational Supplement.

All the way through university you should be observing what's going on in the job market. Download job descriptions and see how your skills match.

Identify what skills you have to develop in order to allow you to apply for that position.

It is also recommended that you post your profile onto a professional networking site for example Linkedin.

This is a networking site only aimed at business and is useful for connecting to people in similar roles to the ones you aspire to or to potential employers. It is extremely popular and very professional. It features jobs and will recommend jobs to you within your profile. Find groups that have interests aligned to your chosen career and read and join in the discussions. This is an excellent way to build up your network of professional people from industry and the business sector.

*** Exercise 29: Career search ***

Complete three jobs searches for the areas you are interested in working in. Download the job descriptions and highlight the key skills and attributes the employer is looking for. State how you already match those skills, or what you need to go and do to acquire more experience. eg. this might involve some work shadowing, or volunteer work.

Find someone who already does the job and ring or email them and ask if they have 10 mins to tell you about the job (the worst they could do is put the phone down or delete your email!).

Researching Possible Employers

It is vital to find out as much as possible about possible employers. This is to help you decide who you'd like to work for and also to help you when you do get an interview.

To start identifying potential employers you first need to think about your future lifestyle. What you need to establish whilst you are doing your degree is how flexible you are about travelling to work and where will you be living? Will you be going back to your home town on completion of your degree? Do you want to travel with your work? Would you like to work in another country?

Use all your vacations to gain as much experience in your chosen field, work experience, work shadowing or volunteering to go and work inside a company. You may have to work for free; this again shows willingness and shows the employer you are worth employing. Make a list of all your ideal employers where you would like to see yourself working, and then focus in on a few to investigate further.

When you apply to each company make sure you spend some time researching what they do and where they are located.

Case study: Losing a job by not researching and not being on time

There is a company that uses an unusual style of recruiting. They invite about 15 people to come at 7.30 am for an interview. At 7.30 they lock the doors - this usually gets them down to 9. They then ask each person to tell them something about the company. Unbelievably they usually send another 4 home at this point. People have turned up for a job interview not knowing anything about the company.

Have a look at the interview episodes of the TV programme The Apprentice on youtube there is nearly always one of them who can't say what the company does.

*** Exercise 30: Researching potential employers. ***

Make a database (spreadsheet programmes like excel can be used) of names, addresses, websites and any information you find out in your research of companies or institutions you would like to work for.

Your tutors may be able to help you with this, or your university careers center. The careers center should have access to graduate directories.

Then do some research about each company. Find out:

➢ What does the company do?
➢ Look at their recent annual report to check how well they are doing.
➢ Where are they based?
➢ What is the structure of the company (what departments are there)?
➢ What is the history of the company or institution?
➢ What types of jobs might be available for future promotion?
➢ Who is the managing director and what is their background?
➢ How many graduates might they take on each year?
➢ Do they have a graduate training programme?
➢ Does it feel like you'd fit in?

Curriculum Vitae (CV)

The world of work is very competitive and you need to make sure your CV sells you. Interviewers can have hundreds of applications so you need to make your CV easy to read, as short as possible and professional looking. As a guideline your CV should be no longer than 2 pages. Make sure at least two other people proofread it for you, preferably someone who has experience of job selection or staff in the careers department. A good tip is to use a table to lay out the information but have the grid lines hidden, that way it is easy to line up everything. Use bold and larger fonts for emphasis, not underlining as it is seen as old fashioned. Do remember as well you may get googled so check out your online presence and perhaps even consider having a blog or website with further information about yourself.

Example of the contents of a good CV

Name

Address

Tel no.   **Email address**

Personal Profile

This is a statement that describes your qualities in about six lines only for example:-

A hard working, totally trustworthy business/ sport media/ nursing graduate with the ability to work as part of a team or independently. Extensive experience working with children within a sport/media/ hospital setting. Flexible, confident and determined to achieve desired goals and outcomes.

Education

Name of University   Degree and grade
Other significant subjects you have studied on your degree programme.
Name of School/College
Subjects studied to A'level with grades.
Subjects studied to GCSE with grades (always list maths and English first)

Work History

Name of Company month/ year to month/ year. You usually put these in order of most recent first going to the most distant but if you have had a significant role that will impress the interviewer put it near the top of the list.

Achievements

Write down anything that you are proud of, for example:

First team rugby captain
Travelled extensively around Europe and Asia.
Worked in New Zealand
Represented the school in overseas exchange programme.

Key Skills

Analysis, research, problem solving, time management etc. State how you have achieved these skills through your degree programme, perhaps give specific examples.

IT

State the different information technology programmes that you have become proficient in using at university. These might include word, excel, SPSS for statistics, data bases, web design etc.

Interpersonal skills

State how you have either stayed motivated or motivated others on your course. State how you have developed your skills to become a team player. Have you got examples of your leadership skills, sales or negotiating skills?

Interests

List all your hobbies and activities you are interested in.

Referees

Do not put references on request. Usually giving two referees is sufficient. Ask permission before giving a referee's details.

Name	Name
Position	Position

Address	Address
Postcode	Postcode
Tel no.	Tel no.
email address	email address.

It is a really good idea to invest in some good quality cream paper to print your CV onto as it makes your CV stand out from all the rest when you apply for a post.

Make sure you really sell yourself on your CV, especially your skills as this is what employers are interested in. You should have a standard version but be prepared to add extra bits or change the order to fit the needs of the employer.

Here are some key words to try and use in your personal summaries and c.v's

Achieved	Administered	Analyzed	Built
Capable	Competent	Consistent	Controlled
Created	Designed	Delivered	Developed
Directed	Economical	Efficient	Enabled
Engineered	Established	Expanded	Experienced
Guided	Implemented	Improved	Initiated
Led	Managed	Organized	Participated
Positive	Processed	Produced	Productive
Proficient	Profitable	Promoted	Qualified
Repaired	Resourceful	Sold	Specialized
Stable	Successful	Supervized	Trained
Versatile	Wide		

*** Exercise 31: Curriculum Vitae ***

Using the template above to create an up-to-date CV that you could send to an employer.

Notes:

....

....

....

....

....

....

....

....

....

....

....

....

Case Study: Being realistic

Michael is a semi-professional football player for local team, potential earnings £700 per week. He's now in the third year of university.

Michael is realistic and knows that he will not make a professional football player, even though this was his childhood dream. He has long term injury problems with his knee and this stops him progressing any further. Michael does not want to move too far away, on completion of his degree, as he would still like to play for his team. Now as Michael is in his final year at university he has to realistically consider his future. Michael has started to apply for local graduate positions. He has been to the careers department at his university to obtain a copy of the graduate directories that are available free of charge to students. These directories advertise all the graduate positions all around the country.

Michael has updated his CV and has a standard covering letter ready to send out to employers.

He has had these documents checked by his personal tutor and Michael is now concentrating on achieving good grades for the modules he is studying so that he can achieve the 2:1 degree classification. This is also required for the positions he would like to apply for. Michael in the meantime is also attending a primary school one morning a week listening to children read and work shadowing primary school teachers as this will keep Michael's further options open for the future if he would like to pursue a career in teaching.

Final words

It is hoped that you have found this book really useful. If you've enjoyed the book please do post reviews on your favorite book sellers site. Thank you for taking the time to read the book.

Now as you have worked your way through the book, you should have a much clearer idea about how to prepare yourself for going to university.

Even though the cost of your degree may be a daunting prospect, the actual achievement on obtaining you degree can be such a gratification for all your hard work. It shows employers that you have invested time, money and effort into your future. Lots of employers will employ you on a graduate level instead of on a trainee level.

You may want to further your studies at Masters level once you have your undergraduate degree. Your options are limitless. Post graduate study is becoming more and more popular. Once you become established within a company they may help to finance you to complete a post graduate course or further continuous professional development.

Every year there is a directory that is available through your local careers department which advertises graduate job opportunities that are available for undergraduate students to apply for. As soon as you start at university make contact with your careers department to see what is available for you. More often the careers department will support you for one year after you complete your course at the university.

Good luck with your preparation for university. I hope this book can help you to make the right choice.

Best Wishes

Angela

Notes:

Universe of Learning Books

"The purpose of learning is growth, and our minds, unlike our bodies, can continue growing as we continue to live." Mortimer Adler

About the publishers

Universe of Learning Limited is a small publisher based in the UK with production in England, Australia and America. Our authors are all experienced trainers or teachers who have taught their skills for many years. We are actively seeking qualified authors and if you visit the authors section on www.uolearn.com you can find out how to apply.

If you are interested in any of our current authors coming to speak at your event please email them through the author section of the uolearn site.

If you would like to purchase larger numbers of books then please do contact us (sales@uolearn. com). We give discounts from 5 books upwards. For larger volumes we can also quote for changes to the cover to accommodate your company logo and to the interior to brand it for your company.

All our books are written by teachers, trainers or people well experienced in their roles and our goal is to help people develop their skills with a well structured range of exercises.

If you have any feedback about this book or other topics that you'd like to see us cover please do contact us at support@uolearn.com.

To buy the printed books please order from your favourite bookshop, including Amazon, Waterstones, Blackwells and Barnes and Noble. For ebooks please visit www.uolearn.com.

Keep Learning!

Developing Your Assertiveness Skills

ISBN: 978-1-84937-057-8, from www.uolearn.com
- ✓ Recognise different forms of behaviour and identify your dominant behaviour type
- ✓ Find ways to develop your confidence
- ✓ Manage the anxiety associated with handling stressful encounters
- ✓ Use the right words, tone and body language
- ✓ Communicate confidently when you want to say no
- ✓ Prepare for challenging conversations
- ✓ Managing emotions

Report Writing

An easy to follow format for writing reports

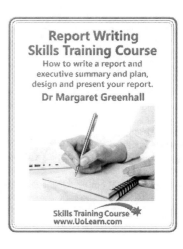

ISBN 978-1-84937-036-3, from www.uolearn.com

This book makes report writing a step by step process for you to follow every time you have a report to write.

- ✓ How to set objectives using 8 simple questions
- ✓ Easy to follow flow chart
- ✓ How to write an executive summary
- ✓ How to layout and structure the report
- ✓ Help people remember what they read

Stress Management

Exercises and techniques to manage stress and anxiety

ISBN: 978-1-84937-002-8, from www.uolearn.com
- ✓ Understand what stress is
- ✓ Become proactive in managing your stress
- ✓ How to become more positive about your life
- ✓ An easy 4 step model to lasting change

Studying for your Future

Skills for life, whilst you study

ISBN: 978-1-84937-047-9, Order at www.uolearn.com

- ✓ A checklist to put together a portfolio to show a prospective employer
- ✓ Learn the skills to prepare you for your degree
- ✓ Help you with literature reviews and writing skills
- ✓ Goal setting to help you focus on your future
- ✓ Sort out your time planning
- ✓ Improve your study skills and exam preparation
- ✓ Prepare for employment

Developing Your Influencing Skills

ISBN: 978-1-84937-004-2, from www.uolearn.com

- ✓ Decide what your influencing goals are
- ✓ Find ways to increase your credibility rating
- ✓ Develop stronger and more trusting relationships
- ✓ Inspire others to follow your lead
- ✓ Become a more influential communicator

Packed with case studies, exercises and practical tips to become more influential.

Dreaming Yourself Aware

Exercises to interpret your dreams

ISBN: 978-1-84937-055-4, Order at www.uolearn.com

- ✓ Learn how to remember and record your dreams
- ✓ Structured approach to understand your dreams
- ✓ A large variety of techniques for dream interpretation
- ✓ Step by step instructions and worked examples
- ✓ Exercises to help you to find answers to problems
- ✓ Understand your motivation and reveal your goals
- ✓ Make positive changes to your life

Dreaming yourself aware gives a step by step guide to interpreting your dreams.

Coaching Skills Training Course

Business and life coaching techniques for

ISBN: 978-1-84937-019-6, from www.uolearn.com
- ✓ An easy to follow 5 step model
- ✓ Learn to both self-coach and coach others
- ✓ Over 25 ready to use ideas
- ✓ Goal setting tools to help achieve ambitions

A toolbox of ideas to help you become a great coach.

Successful Minute Taking

How to prepare, write and organise agendas and minutes of meetings

ISBN 978-1-84937-040-0, from www.uolearn.com

- ✓ Becoming more confident in your role
- ✓ A checklist of what to do
- ✓ Learn what to include in minutes

Learn to be an excellent meeting secretary.

Practical and Effective Performance Management

ISBN: 978-1-84937-037-0, from www.uolearn.com
- ✓ Five key ideas to understanding performance
- ✓ A clear four step model
- ✓ Key what works research that is practical
- ✓ A large, wide ranging choice of tools
- ✓ Practical exercises and action planning for managers

A toolbox of ideas to help you become a better leader.

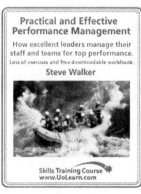

Speed Writing

ISBN 978-1-84937-011-0, from www.uolearn.com
Easy exercises to learn faster writing in just 6 hours.

- ✓ "The principles are very easy to follow, and I am already using it to take notes."
- ✓ "I will use this system all the time."
- ✓ "Your system is so easy to learn and use."

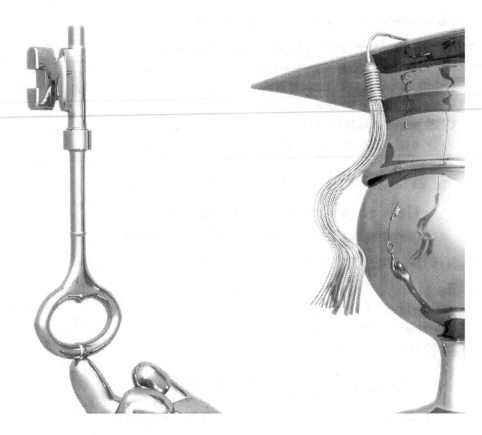

"Don't live down to expectations.
Go out there and do something remarkable."
Wendy Wasserstein